VOLCANOES

First published in Great Britain in 2000 by
Colin Baxter Photography Ltd
Grantown-on-Spey
PH26 3NA
Scotland
www.worldlifelibrary.co.uk

Text © Peter Clarkson 2000
Illustrations © Richard Garratt 2000
WorldLife Library Series
A CIP Catalogue record for this book is available from the British Library.

ISBN 1-84107-063-7

Photographs © 2000:

Front cover © Nicholas Devore / Tony Stone Images
Page 1 © Tui De Roy / Oxford Scientific Films
Page 4 © Pacific Stock / Bruce Coleman Collection
Page 6 © Orion Press / Bruce Coleman Collection
Page 9 © Hjalmar R Bardarson / Oxford Scientific Films
Page 12 © Mary Plage / Bruce Coleman Collection
Page 13 © Hjalmar R Bardarson / Oxford Scientific Films
Page 14 © Bruce Davidson / BBC Natural History Unit
Page 18 © Klaus Nigge / BBC Natural History Unit
Page 20 © Richard Coomber / Planet Earth Pictures
Page 21 © Gerald S Cubitt / Bruce Coleman Collection
Page 22 © Jeff Foott / Bruce Coleman Collection
Page 24 © Michael Pitts / Oxford Scientific Films
Page 25 © Jeff Foott / Bruce Coleman Collection
Page 26 © Otto Hahn / Still Pictures
Page 27 © Stephen and Donna O'Meara / Planet Earth Pictures
Page 28 © Doug Allan / Oxford Scientific Films
Page 31 © Colin Baxter
Page 35 © Peter Galloway
Page 36 © NASA / Oxford Scientific Films
Page 39 © Colin Baxter
Page 40 © Vincent Bretagnolle / Still Pictures
Page 41 © Derek Croucher / Bruce Coleman Collection

Page 42 © Pacific Stock / Bruce Coleman Collection
Page 45 © Pacific Stock / Bruce Coleman Collection
Page 47 © Tui De Roy / Oxford Scientific Films
Page 50 © John Marshall / Tony Stone Images
Page 51 © Krafft, I & V / Planet Earth Pictures
Page 53 © Kevin Schafer / NHPA
Page 54 © Dieter and Mary Plage / Oxford Scientific Films
Page 56 © NASA / Oxford Scientific Films
Page 57 a © Michael W Richards / Oxford Scientific Films
Page 57 b © Doug Allan / BBC Natural History Unit
Page 57 c © Charles Tyler / Oxford Scientific Films
Page 57 d © Breck P Kent / Earth Scenes
Page 58 © James Balog / Tony Stone Images
Page 61 © Pacific Stock / Bruce Coleman Collection
Page 62 © Krafft, I & V / Planet Earth Pictures
Page 65 © Colin Baxter
Page 66 © NASA / Oxford Scientific Films
Page 67 © Alberto Nardi / NHPA
Page 69 © Chuck Pefley / Tony Stone Images
Page 70 © Durieux, I & V / Planet Earth Pictures
Page 72 © Harold E Wilson / Oxford Scientific Films
Back cover © D. Decobecq / Still Pictures

Front Cover Photograph: Villarrica, Chile and Lanin, Argentina.
Page 1 Photograph: The 1996 eruption of Mount Ruapehu in New Zealand.
Page 4 Photograph: Very hot and very fluid pahoehoe lava from Kilauea on the Big Island, Hawaii.
Page 72 Photograph: Shishaldin volcano on Uminak Island, Alaska, United States.
Back Cover Photograph: Eruption of Mount Etna, Sicily.

Printed in China

VOLCANOES

Peter Clarkson

Colin Baxter Photography Ltd, Grantown-on-Spey, Scotland

Contents

Introduction

Volcano! Just the mention of the word creates a mental picture, which varies with the listener's own perception. An artist may think of the classical shape of Mount Fuji; a historian may recall the destruction of Pompeii by Vesuvius; a geologist may speculate about the gas content of the lava in relation to its viscosity; a newspaper editor may see the scope for spectacular photographs and stories of human suffering and heroism that will boost newspaper circulation. Whatever thoughts spring to mind, nobody can be but impressed by the awful power of a volcanic eruption and the devastation that may be caused.

In July 1963 a trip to Iceland opened my eyes to all manner of volcanic phenomena. I marveled at real volcanic craters; bubbling springs of boiling mud; hot pools that suddenly drained for a few seconds before exploding vertically in a geyser; streams flowing from beneath glaciers with sulfur-coated rocks in their beds, indicating thermal activity under the ice. My enthusiasm knew no bounds, but, unfortunately, I had not seen a volcano erupt. As we returned to Britain on MV *Gullfoss*, I little realised that the volcano Surtsey would emerge above the sea immediately below where the ship had sailed barely three months earlier. Two years later I returned to Iceland for a longer trip. At the end of this trip eight of us pooled our remaining money to charter a light aircraft for a flight around Surtsey. The main crater had a red glow but was largely quiet, while the new island of Little Surtsey was exploding continuously. A small cone of ash had been breached by the sea on one side and, as each new wave flowed into the crater, the volcano responded with an explosive ejection of ash and rock mixed with a cloud of steam. I remember feeling warm inside the aircraft but I suspect this was excitement rather than temperature. The excursion confirmed beyond any doubt that I wanted to be a geologist and that the flight to Surtsey should not be a once-in-a-lifetime experience.

What are volcanoes? Where and why do they happen? The aim of this book is to answer these questions and to explain one of the great natural wonders of the Earth.

Mount Fuji or 'Fuji-san' in Japan is a near-perfect volcanic cone, cloaked in snow.

Anyone who has seen a volcano in eruption will be overawed by the display of immense power that the Earth exhibits. The column of smoke may rise several miles into the atmosphere; streams of lava may flow down the mountainside burning everything in their paths; explosive activity may remove a large part of the original structure of the mountain by reducing it to dust that is shot into the air. Rocks as large as houses may be thrown hundreds of feet into the air and a blanket of ash may settle over the land, burning and suffocating all life beneath its pall. Volcanoes also allow the various facets of nature to demonstrate their persistence, as plants and animals return to colonize the land despite its almost complete sterilization by the eruption.

In 1840, Sir James Clark Ross commanded an expedition to search for the south magnetic pole. With his two small ships, he was the first person to break through the pack ice of the Ross Sea and reach the coast of that part of Antarctica. The sight of a plume of smoke trailing from the summit of a snow-clad mountain set in a land of perpetual snow and ice was incomprehensible to him. How could such a source of heat occur in such a cold place? Geological science has advanced enormously since that time and there is nothing unusual in such a setting because the heat of the volcano comes from deep within the Earth, whereas the snow and ice are the products of climate and the atmosphere. Indeed, sub-glacial volcanoes are now well known, particularly in Iceland, where such eruptions melt enormous volumes of ice that eventually escape from beneath the glacier to pour across the surrounding plains in spectacular floods called 'glacier bursts'.

Each volcano is unique and largely unpredictable. Many have been dormant throughout human history and regarded as benign, only to erupt suddenly with little warning to catch the local population unawares. Such events may no longer surprise geologists, who now use sophisticated analytical techniques to date rocks and show that some volcanoes slumber for thousands of years before bursting into life again. Volcanoes have been active since the Earth began to cool almost 4500 million years ago and have occupied a central role in forming the planet. They will continue to do so for hundreds of millions of years to come.

Pahoehoe lava on Surtsey, Iceland, building the island once the eruption emerged above sea level.

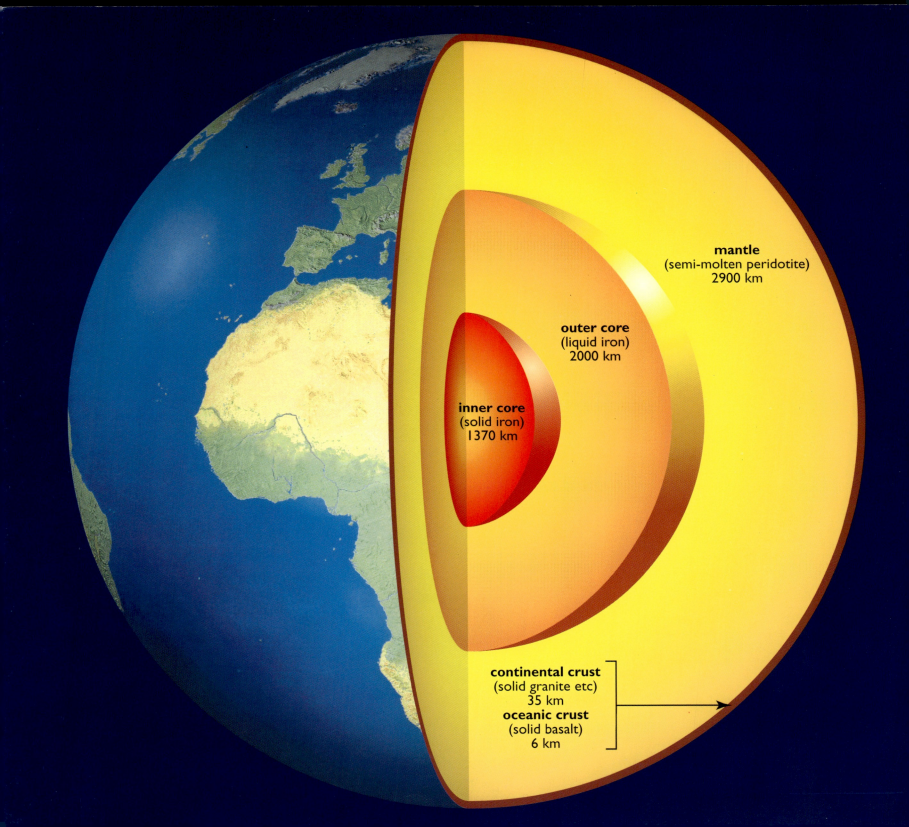

mantle
(semi-molten peridotite)
2900 km

outer core
(liquid iron)
2000 km

inner core
(solid iron)
1370 km

continental crust
(solid granite etc)
35 km

oceanic crust
(solid basalt)
6 km

What are Volcanoes?

Structure of the Earth

The Earth was formed about 4500 million years ago as a molten mass orbiting the Sun. Gradually the Earth began to cool and as it did so, it separated into several parts under the force of gravity. The heaviest materials sank towards the center of the spinning globe while the lighter materials floated upwards. The Earth today comprises three major parts: the core, the mantle and the crust. The core has a solid center, probably formed largely of iron, surrounded by an outer core of liquid iron and some silicates. The core is the Earth's internal heat source. Eddy currents in the outer core are the source of the Earth's magnetic field. Above the core is the mantle, composed of a heavy, dark rock called peridotite. The mantle is hot and exists in a semi-molten state which means that convection currents can move very slowly, rising from the hotter lower levels towards the crust then turning and cooling as they flow beneath the crust before finally sinking down again. The crust of the Earth is of two types, the lighter continental crust that forms most of the land surface and the denser oceanic crust that underlies all the oceans.

The relative sizes of the components of the Earth are shown opposite, where it can be seen that the component with the largest volume is the mantle, and this is the most important part in relation to volcanoes. The temperature of the mantle is about 2400°F (1300°C), it increases with greater depth and this temperature gradient drives convection within the mantle. Where the semi-molten mantle rises under the mid-ocean ridges, the pressure gradually reduces and allows part of the mantle to melt, forming magma that moves upwards and erupts as lava on the sea floor. If the eruption continues for long enough the lavas will eventually emerge above the surface of the ocean and form volcanic islands. In some cases, for reasons not yet understood, the source of the melting lies at the core–mantle boundary and such cases are called hot

A cut-away diagram of the Earth showing its principal components.

spots. These hot spots appear to be stationary, relative to the core, and have a lifespan of many millions of years. Geologists are able to distinguish hot-spot volcanoes from other oceanic volcanoes by the different compositions of the lavas.

Most continental volcanoes lie along the margin of continents. The heat of the mantle does play a part in the formation of these volcanoes but there are other heating effects. Together these lead to melting of rock at the base of the continental crust and this molten rock rises and accumulates in vast reservoirs within the crust. Gradually the pressure in these reservoirs increases to a point where the crust is no longer able to contain the magma and it escapes upwards and erupts on the surface to form volcanoes. The incorporation of crustal material by the magma in its upward travel means that the lavas have a different composition from both types of oceanic volcanoes. All volcanoes have one aspect in common, they result from the release of pressure on the molten magma. To this extent, a volcano may be compared to the safety valve on a pressure cooker; once the surrounding rocks can no longer contain the pressure of the magma it is released through an eruption.

The eruption column of Anak Krakatoa, Indonesia.

Mount Hekla, one of the highest mountains in Iceland, has a long history of volcanic activity since Iceland was first settled in the ninth century AD, erupting 20 times during the last 1100 years. Lava can be seen flowing down the snow-covered slopes from the crater.

An eruption of Kimanura volcano in the Virunga National Park, Zaire.
A very fluid lava containing a high gas content produces spectacular fountains in the crater.
Lava escaping from the crater flows rapidly downhill before slowing as it cools.

Where are Volcanoes?

Plate Tectonics

In 1908, Alfred Wegener, a German physicist and meteorologist, noticed the remarkable similarity in the shapes of the opposing coastlines of the Atlantic Ocean. He showed that if you slid the eastern coastline of the Americas towards the western coastlines of Europe and Africa you could achieve a remarkably good fit, like a jigsaw. He suggested that these continental masses had been joined together at some time in the past and had separated by an unknown process that he called continental drift. Just as geologists in earlier times had difficulty persuading people that the Earth must have been created much earlier than 4004 BC, so Wegener's theory did not enjoy widespread acceptance. It was not until the 1960s, when two scientists, Frederick Vine and Drummond Matthews from Cambridge University in England, discovered mirror-image magnetic patterns in the oceanic crust across the Mid-Atlantic Ridge southwest of Iceland, that it was possible to see a mechanism for moving the continents.

It was well known that the Mid-Atlantic Ridge represented a line of volcanic activity with volcanic islands, such as Tristan da Cunha and Iceland, along its length. The lava that formed the ridge had been erupted from the underlying mantle onto the sea floor and as it cooled, the magnetic minerals in the lava aligned themselves with the Earth's magnetic field at that time. It was also known that the Earth's magnetic field reverses from time to time as the North and South magnetic poles swap positions. Vine and Matthews showed their results on a map with the normal and reversely magnetized rocks depicted as black and white stripes. They argued that these recorded a history of continued lava eruption from the ridge and by dating samples from the sea floor they were able to show the rate of movement. This became known as 'sea-floor spreading' and was the foundation of what we now know as the theory of plate tectonics.

Convection currents in the mantle drag the overlying continents or plates with them as they flow along beneath the surface of the Earth, and the gap that would be created behind the edge of the plate is filled by new lava from the mantle to form new oceanic crust. If new oceanic crust is constantly being formed in one area then it must be somehow consumed in another area. At present, as the Atlantic Ocean grows wider, so the Pacific Ocean is slowly shrinking as the oceanic crust dips under the western seaboard of the Americas and disappears back into the mantle. In other areas we find that one continental plate is actually colliding with another. This is the case with the Indian sub-continent, which has moved northward with time until it collided with southern Asia. Here the crust of the continents has been crumpled to form the highest mountains on the Earth, the Himalayas. There are other types of plate margin and some of these are illustrated in the diagram.

There are two main types of activity that take place along plate margins: earthquakes and volcanic eruptions. Where a convection current drags the oceanic crust back into the mantle beneath a continental margin, it is called a subduction zone. Friction develops between the down-going slab of oceanic crust and the overlying continental crust in a subduction zone. Stress accumulates in the rocks as these movements progress, and eventually the rocks can no longer absorb any more strain and they break as their positions re-adjust. When this happens an earthquake occurs. Farther down in the subduction zone the frictional heating starts to melt the rocks and the hotter, less dense magma begins to rise within the crust and may eventually break through the surface as a volcano.

Geologists have shown that plate tectonic activity has been a continuing process since the Earth's crust was first formed. The thick continental crust has been continually broken apart into separate plates that have drifted, collided, and amalgamated while oceanic crust has been subducted. About 200 million years ago there was only one major continent, known as Pangea. The Atlantic, Indian and Antarctic or Southern oceans did not exist and the ancestral Pacific Ocean surrounded Pangea. It is not known why Pangea began to split apart along the Atlantic and in the Indian and Southern oceans but it began to do so and gradually started to form the continents that we know today. The process of sea-floor spreading that generated new oceanic crust and the destruction of existing oceanic crust means that there is virtually no oceanic crust on Earth that is more than about 200 million years old.

A schematic diagram of the Earth's crust, showing volcano origins in relation to plate tectonics.

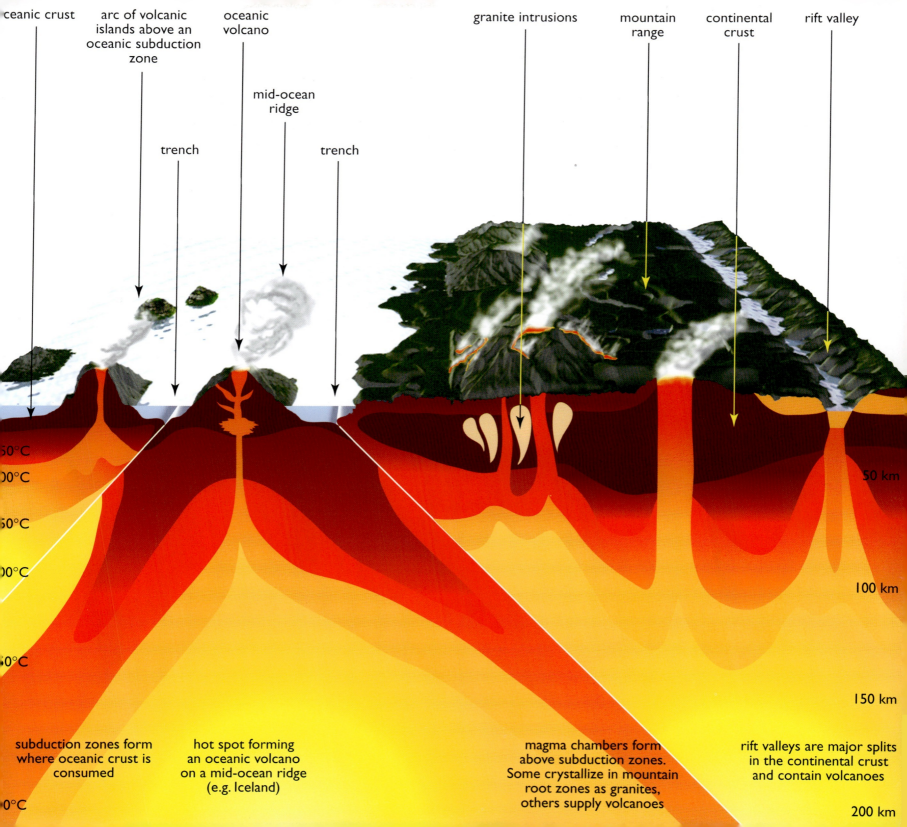

ceanic crust

arc of volcanic islands above an oceanic subduction zone

oceanic volcano

mid-ocean ridge

trench

trench

granite intrusions

mountain range

continental crust

rift valley

50°C

00°C

50°C

00°C

50 km

60°C

100 km

0°C

150 km

200 km

subduction zones form where oceanic crust is consumed

hot spot forming an oceanic volcano on a mid-ocean ridge (e.g. Iceland)

magma chambers form above subduction zones. Some crystallize in mountain root zones as granites, others supply volcanoes

rift valleys are major splits in the continental crust and contain volcanoes

An aerial view of an eruption of Karymsky volcano in Kamchatka, Russia.
Kamchatka lies along the northwestern margin of the Pacific Ocean where there is active
subduction of the oceanic crust, giving rise to a long line of volcanoes.

The Pacific 'Ring of Fire'

The Pacific Ocean is very slowly shrinking in size as the Atlantic Ocean continues to widen, so that Pacific Ocean crust has somehow to be consumed. This is happening around most of the boundary of the Pacific Ocean by subduction. In the west this is happening beneath New Zealand, northward through the islands of Indonesia, and along the Japanese islands to the Kamchatka Peninsula of eastern Russia. Across the Bering Strait the same thing is happening along the Aleutian Islands, southward down the western coasts of Alaska, Canada and North America, past Mexico and Central America to Venezuela, Peru and Chile and then even into the Antarctic Peninsula. There are volcanoes all around the Pacific Ocean, some of them active, many of them dormant and some extinct. A few of these have provided some of the most spectacular eruptions of recent times; Mount St Helens in the Cascade Range of North America in 1980; Mount Pinatubo in the Philippines in 1991; Katmai in the Aleutian Islands in 1908; and many others.

The eruptions of these volcanoes have some common features because they are all generated by basically the same process, subduction of oceanic crust. A common type of lava is called andesite, named after the Andes Mountains in South America where these rocks were first described. These eruptions tend to be very violent and relatively short-lived before the volcano becomes dormant again, sometimes for thousands of years before its next eruption. Molten andesite is a fairly viscous lava that does not flow very easily. Consequently, the increasing pressure in the magma chamber can often be contained for a long time before an eruption finally occurs, but when it does, it does so explosively, with dramatic effect. Lava is produced but the main effect is normally one of enormous clouds of dust and ash that may be ejected to tremendous heights, and are then carried by the wind to settle over vast areas of the surrounding countryside. Some of these volcanoes are in sparsely populated mountain regions, such as the Rocky Mountains and the Andes of the Americas, where they cause relatively little damage to towns and villages. These volcanoes are in marked contrast to those of Indonesia and Japan where many are close to major centers of population and cause widespread damage and human suffering.

Supervolcanoes

In 1971 a geologist in Nebraska, looking to see if recent rains had exposed any new fossil localities, was amazed to find some 200 fossilized rhinoceroses and many other animals. All had died in the prime of life from a sudden catastrophe about 10 million years ago.

Old Faithful geyser.

He thought that a volcanic eruption might have been the cause, but there are no volcanoes in Nebraska. Volcanoes of that age are 1000 miles (1600 km) away in southwestern Idaho but research showed that the ash in Nebraska came from the volcano in Idaho. The first supervolcano had been recognized.

No one has ever seen a supervolcanic eruption but the size of the eruption can be calculated from the volume of ash produced. A supervolcanic eruption may be a thousand times more powerful than the eruption of Mount St Helens in 1980. Such enormous eruptions do not leave a classical volcano as witness to their activity. They leave an enormous caldera that is difficult to identify.

Yellowstone Park in northwestern Wyoming is famous for its hot springs, but there is no obvious volcano. The caldera is just too large to be appreciated from the ground and geologists could not see the ancient caldera until a satellite image was available. Radiometric dating showed that the eruptions occurred at about 2, 1.2 and 0.6 million years ago. The vast magma chamber, about 28 by 12 miles (45 by 20 km) in area and about 6 miles (10 km) thick, is growing again beneath the park. If the Yellowstone supervolcano stays with its cycle of eruptions then the fourth one is overdue.

Semeru volcano erupting in Indonesia. Mount Bromo volcano (left foreground) is also active.

Associated Phenomena

Geysers and Hot Springs

Volcanoes are tremendous sources of heat that may persist for thousands of years after the eruptive activity has ceased. This may manifest itself simply as warm ground or as fumaroles (steam vents), hot springs or geysers. The most spectacular of these are geysers, natural fountains of hot water that erupt periodically.

The name geyser is derived from *Geysir* (meaning to 'gush') in Iceland, a thermal area that has produced many geysers for hundreds of years. The original 'geysir' is now dormant, possibly due to clogged plumbing, but adjacent geysers are still very active. The 'plumbing' of geysers can be quite complex but basically groundwater is trapped in an underground chamber where it is super-heated well beyond the normal boiling point of water. Eventually the pressure is released and the water boils instantaneously so that it fountains upwards as it escapes from the chamber. In some geysers this happens as often as once per minute, in others it may be as long as several hours between eruptions. Those geysers that erupt frequently usually produce relatively small fountains, perhaps only 33 ft (10 m) high, but some with a longer periodicity may spout to more than 330 ft (100 m) high. In New Zealand between 1899 and 1904, the Waimangu geyser routinely produced a jet of water 1650 ft (500 m) high and ceased operating only when the groundwater level fell, following the collapse of a natural dam. Once again, the pressure-cooker safety valve analogy can describe a geyser.

Hot springs occur in two broad categories, those springs in areas of siliceous volcanism that are normally clear water, like geysers, and those that are sulfurous and usually consist of boiling mud. The clear water springs still contain quantities of dissolved minerals, especially silica, and these are deposited around the springs as the water cools. Some of these form dazzling white sinter terraces, such as those in Yellowstone National Park in the United States and at Pamukkale in Turkey. In other areas the mineral or algal content colors

Great Fountain geyser and surrounding hot springs in Yellowstone National Park, Wyoming.

the water, often producing beautiful azure pools. Boiling mud pools occur in muddy areas where just walking across a muddy hillside may produce a trail of steaming footprints. The mud may be of various colors, often tinged with yellow due to the high sulfur content, and the temperature of the boiling mud may be above 212°F (100°C). The soft consistency of the mud can make it dangerous to approach too close to such pools.

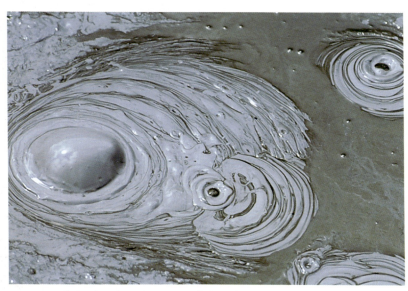

A boiling mud pool at Pokili, Papua New Guinea.

Fumaroles are essentially vents in the ground for the escape of hot gases. These gases may have a variety of compositions as well as steam. One of the commoner gases is carbon dioxide and because this is heavier than air it can collect in hollows in the ground, where it can suffocate animals and people who may be trapped there. Pure sulfur often occurs around fumaroles, having condensed from the escaping gases, and provides a brilliant yellow crust around the vent. Other sulfide minerals may also be deposited and cinnabar (mercury sulfide) leaves a deep red coating on the ground.

Earthquakes

An earthquake is caused when the Earth suddenly adjusts to the release of stress in the rocks. Most major earthquakes occur along faults, natural lines of weakness, in the Earth's crust. The rocks on either side of the fault are trying to move in different directions. At first the natural strength of the rocks will accommodate the stress but when it can no

This geyser in the Great Basin, Nevada, has built a small cone of tufa around its vent.

longer do so the rocks move suddenly with an enormous release of energy that shakes the ground. Many of the strongest earthquakes are related to major faults, called fracture zones, where oceanic crust is being subducted under a continental margin. The famous earthquakes of San Francisco are typical examples.

In a volcanic eruption, large amounts of lava and ash may be erupted so that the rocks beneath the volcano necessarily adapt to the changes in volume created. This inevitably involves the movement of rock masses as the crust adjusts but the amount of movement is usually small and the resulting earthquake is quite minor. Unlike a major earthquake, the damage to buildings and property is likely to be small, certainly compared with the destruction caused by lava and ash from the actual eruption.

Lava fountains at night on Mount Etna, Sicily, Italy.

The formation of a volcanic caldera by the collapse of the original cone and crater of the volcano downward over the drained magma chamber can involve the movement of enormous volumes of rock. Once volcanic activity has ceased, examination of a newly formed caldera can show considerable vertical movement of tens or even hundreds of feet. However, the total movement usually takes place over a period of months, or even years, as a long succession of small slips. In such cases the 'earthquake' of each slip will be very small and may only be detected by sensitive instruments. The explosive eruption of Krakatoa in August 1883 undoubtedly created an earthquake but it did little direct damage; the damage was done by the tsunamis created by the explosion.

Pacaya volcano in Guatemala erupting at dusk. A cloud of steam and volcanic gases hangs over the top of the mountain, obscuring the view of the crater, but its position can be gauged by the lava flowing down from the summit.

The summit of Mount Erebus on Ross Island, Antarctica, with its
telltale plume of smoke and steam being swept away in the wind. The crater
contains a small lava lake that has been active for at least the last 100 years.

Tsunamis

Tsunamis are seismic sea waves caused by disruption of the sea floor. They are commonly known as 'tidal waves' but in fact they have nothing to do with the tides. The disruptions may be caused by earthquakes on the sea floor, major submarine slides (like underwater landslides) or by explosive eruptions of oceanic volcanoes. One of the most famous tsunamis was that caused by the eruption of Krakatoa. The volcanic explosions created several tsunamis that devastated the coasts of the nearby islands of Java and Sumatra, creating waves as high as 100 ft (30 m) in some narrow bays. The death-toll was 36,000. One of these tsunami was identified in the English Channel where it was still 12 in (30 cm) high.

A tsunami is not a dangerous wave in the ocean where the water is deep. The original seismic shock creates the wave that may travel at 625 mph (1000 kmph) in the deep ocean. Although it travels at great speed it may pass a ship unnoticed by those on board because the wave height is so small. However, as it reaches shallower water the advance of the wave is slowed by the decreasing depth of water, and its energy begins to build the height of the wave. When the wave reaches the shore it has become a towering wall of water that crashes onto the land and drives far inland, carrying all before it. Buildings are destroyed, vehicles are tossed and squashed, and small boats have been carried several miles inland from the coast. Tsunamis are particularly destructive where they enter long narrow bays. Here the volume of water is not only forced upward by the shelving sea floor but also by the constraining shores of the bay.

Perhaps the most dangerous aspect of tsunamis is that the damage they cause may happen at huge distances from the source of the disturbance. People living close to a violent eruption will be prepared for a tsunami to strike, but those living thousands of miles away across an ocean will be caught completely unawares. It was for precisely this reason that the Pacific Tsunami Warning Center was established on Hawaii near the center of the Pacific. Here geophysicists monitor earthquake activity recorded by seismometers located all around the Pacific that send data to Hawaii in real time. As soon as an earthquake occurs they can determine its precise location and size measured on the Richter scale. They will use this information to issue a Tsunami Watch, advising all potentially vulnerable places around the Pacific that there could be a tsunami on its way. They keep in close contact with scientists all over the Pacific to determine whether or not a tsunami has been generated. Once a tsunami has been confirmed the Center will issue a Tsunami Warning so that the civil authorities in all the vulnerable places can take the appropriate action. This will normally mean that everyone will be evacuated from low-lying coastal areas so that when the tsunami arrives the loss of life will be kept to a minimum.

Jökulhlaups

When James Clark Ross first saw Mount Erebus on Ross Island in the Antarctic he could not understand how there could be an active volcano in such a cold and icy place. Geologists working in Antarctica have found many volcanoes there, but only their summits project above the ice sheet. These volcanoes are no longer active but the geologists have found that many of the lavas have a structure called pillow lava. Pillow lavas form underwater where the stream of lava flowing into a lake or the sea is rapidly cooled and forms small balls of lava, up to 3 ft (1 m) in diameter. They have a chilled crust although they are still very hot inside and can deform easily. They accumulate in enormous piles, as the lava continues to advance, and the balls flatten under the weight of the overlying lava balls. They now look like pillows and each one may develop a distinctive keel as the bottom of it is compressed into the gap between the pillows beneath it. Some divers, with the courage to swim close to a lava flow as it enters the sea, have observed pillows being formed.

When a volcano erupts under an ice sheet it melts enormous amounts of ice. At first the water is contained by the weight of the overlying ice but gradually, under pressure, it spreads and forces its way outwards between the base of the ice and the bedrock. As it approaches the edge of the ice sheet the pressure of the water reaches a point at which the ice can no longer contain it and the water bursts forth. The enormous power of the water carries huge blocks of ice and a tremendous amount of sediment scoured from the bed of the ice sheet and the land of its outwash plain. Such 'glacier bursts' are also known as *jökulhlaups*, the word used to describe these in Iceland where they have been particularly well documented.

An eruption of Grimsvötn beneath the Vatnajökul ice cap in southeast Iceland. This volcano erupts periodically and, if the eruption is large enough, it may cause a jökulhlaup *that floods across the coastal plain down to the sea. The heat of the eruption melts enormous quantities of ice at the base of the ice sheet. In the initial stages of the eruption this water will be contained by the overlying ice. As the eruption continues and more ice is melted, the growing pressure forces the water downhill between the ice and the bedrock until it eventually bursts from beneath the edge of the ice sheet. The sudden release of water carries with it huge blocks of ice and scours deep channels across the coastal plain as the water rushes to the sea. Nobody lives in this area between the ice cap and the sea because any buildings would be swept away. There is a coast road across the area with bridges over the glacial outwash streams but many of these are often destroyed by the* jökulhlaup *when the volcano erupts. The last of these* jökulhlaups *was in 1998, about one month after the start of the eruption.*

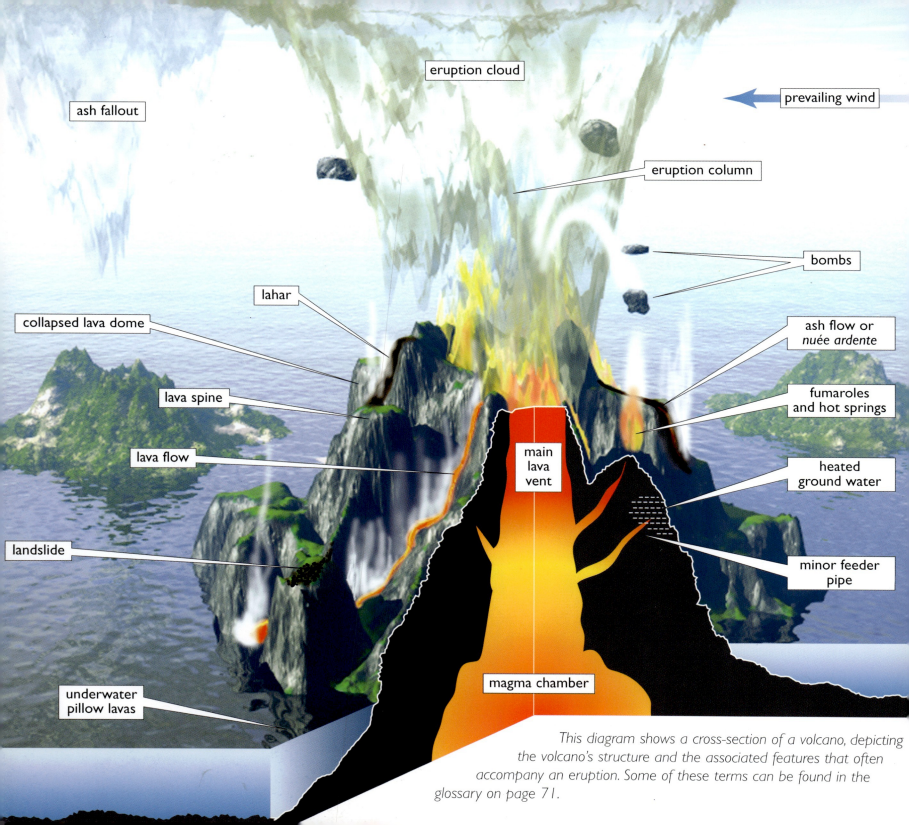

eruption cloud

prevailing wind

ash fallout

eruption column

bombs

lahar

collapsed lava dome

ash flow or *nuée ardente*

lava spine

fumaroles and hot springs

lava flow

main lava vent

heated ground water

landslide

minor feeder pipe

magma chamber

underwater pillow lavas

This diagram shows a cross-section of a volcano, depicting the volcano's structure and the associated features that often accompany an eruption. Some of these terms can be found in the glossary on page 71.

Volcanic Hazards and Benefits

Direct Destruction

The immediate products of a volcanic eruption are lava, ash and gas, but not every eruption produces all of these. Geologists studying volcanoes can determine from the rocks forming the volcano what is the most common product of that particular volcano. Such knowledge can be very helpful in determining the likely product of an imminent eruption, which is very useful when issuing warnings and advising evacuation of the local area.

Lava is always hot and will burn whatever it touches. The degree of danger depends to a large extent on the type of lava and its temperature. Basaltic lavas, such as those on the Hawaiian islands, are very hot, up to 2200°F (1200°C), and very fluid. They can flow at very high speeds, as much as 30 mph (50 kmph), and reach more than 6 miles (10 km) from the crater but they are usually well constrained by the existing topography. Nevertheless, the lava will destroy everything in its path.

Volcanic ash is the most widespread and destructive product of an eruption. A major explosive eruption will send a column of ash thousands of feet into the atmosphere, where it will be carried by the wind to fall over huge areas, often at great distances from the actual volcano. Most of the ash will fall close to the volcano, blanketing the area with many feet of hot cinders. These suffocate all life and may completely bury nearby buildings. Even some distance from the volcano the sheer weight of ash, in places where it is just three feet thick, will crush roofs and collapse buildings. Although the fall-out of ash may cause widespread damage, the most dangerous ash eruption is the *nuée ardente*, a French expression coined by geologist Alfred Lacroix, meaning a glowing cloud. It is actually an incandescent mixture of gas, ash and rock fragments that acts like a low viscosity fluid. It can flow much faster and farther than lava, leaving no time for escape. *Nuée ardentes* from Mount Vesuvius were responsible for the destruction of the Roman towns of Pompeii and Herculaneum in AD 79.

The commonest gases produced in volcanic eruptions are carbon dioxide, sulfur dioxide and water vapor. On their own, these gases rarely do much damage, except where large volumes of carbon dioxide flood natural hollows in the surrounding countryside and suffocate all life. However, it is the sudden release of the gases in a lava that provides much of the explosive energy of any eruption.

Indirect Destruction

One of the most destructive effects of an eruption can be the lahar or mud flow. When there is a large quantity of water available it mixes with the ash and soil on the side of the volcano and pours down the flanks like a river of mud. Such lahars can destroy whole towns, flooding them to a depth of several feet in mud that then sets hard. Often a high volcano will be snow-capped but the heat of the eruption melts the snow and gives rise to a lahar. An eruption of Nevado del Ruiz in the Colombian Andes in 1845 created a lahar that destroyed a village and its 1000 inhabitants. The new town of Armero was built over the lahar. In November 1985 a minor eruption of Ruiz melted its ice cap and the resulting lahar destroyed the town and this time more than 20,000 people died.

Earthquakes associated with volcanic eruptions are usually relatively small and do not result in much damage. However, they may trigger other events that can be very destructive. Landslips and avalanches may happen and do far more damage than the eruption itself. They can travel considerable distances and affect areas that would normally be regarded as relatively safe from an eruption. Villages or towns in valleys below a volcano can be prime targets.

When a coastal or island volcano erupts, an earthquake may trigger a major submarine slide. In itself, this may do no damage of concern to people but such marine slides may cause a tsunami. Again, this may be of little concern to people nearby the volcano but the long-range effect of a tsunami can be disastrous thousands of miles away across the ocean. This is especially the case around the shores of the Pacific Ocean.

Direct Advantages

Deposits of volcanic ash are very rich in mineral nutrients and form particularly fertile soils. In tropical regions, plants and animals will very quickly colonize ash deposits and the

The first recorded eruption of the Soufrière Hills of Montserrat in the West Indies began in July 1995 and, by comparison with other Caribbean volcanoes, is potentially very dangerous. A pyroclastic flow has buried the streets of the town in ash to a depth of more than a meter.

landscape is restored to a cover of dense tropical vegetation. On the Italian island of Sicily there are extensive vineyards on the flanks of Mount Etna. The reason is that the rich volcanic soil is excellent for growing vines and regularly provides good grape harvests. The price that the farmers have to pay for this bounty is that from time to time a new eruption may destroy their farms. On the other hand, a light dusting of volcanic ash can be a good natural fertilizer as the rains leach the mineral content from the ash into the soil.

Many volcanoes produce mineral concentrations of different kinds and these may be sufficiently large to be worked as commercial deposits. Sulfur is produced in enormous quantities by some volcanoes. The highest mine in the world, at 19,685 ft (6000 m) above sea level in the Andes of northern Chile, is a sulfur mine. Other Chilean volcanoes produce borax which is extensively mined. The very light, aerated lava called pumice can be worked for a building stone, is used in cement production and also as an industrial abrasive, as well as the pumice stones commonly found in bathrooms.

A relatively recent discovery has been the so-called 'black smokers' that occur deep in the central rift of active mid-ocean ridges. These are the sites for the generation of new oceanic crust as the adjacent plates move apart. Hot springs, at temperatures as high as 662°F (350°C), bubble up from the ocean floor, rich in metal sulfide minerals that are deposited on the sides of the vent. Gradually these vents build tall chimneys that continue to belch out black mineral-rich waters, hence their name. Most surprising of all was the variety of life forms – crabs, clams, worms and bacteria – that survive around the smokers, dependent entirely on the volcanic heat and gases for sustenance.

It is perhaps worth recalling that virtually all life and resources of the world owe their ultimate origin to the Earth and mostly to igneous activity in one form or another. Some of the world's major mineral deposits were originally formed by volcanic activity but earth movements, plate tectonics and metamorphism have changed their original settings and concentrations to produce the deposits that have been brought closer to the surface and exposed by erosion.

A satellite image of Mount Etna on the island of Sicily, Italy.

Geothermal Power

The Earth is a giant thermal engine releasing heat from the core outwards through the mantle and the crust. It is now generally accepted that the energy released by the decay of the radioactive elements uranium, thorium and potassium is the primary source of the heat flow. Geophysicists can measure this with sensitive instruments at any point but the areas of highest heat flow are inevitably linked to volcanic areas. These are the geothermal areas where this energy can be used. The simplest use is cooking in pools of boiling water, something that explorers may still do to conserve fuel supplies. However, modern man has employed technology to exploit this free energy source in much more sophisticated ways. In Reykjavik, natural hot water has been tapped since 1925 for use in houses throughout the city. Today, much of the water has to be pumped but its temperature has not changed. This is an essential energy source for Iceland, which has no supplies of coal, oil or natural gas. Natural hot water is also exploited in many other parts of the world and not just by man. In northern Japan, the indigenous macaque monkeys have learned to bathe in hot springs to make the winter temperatures of -4°F (-20°C) more bearable.

Heat is one form of energy that can be converted into other forms and may be used for power generation. Hot water, at temperatures as high as 662°F (350°C), can be tapped and converted to steam to drive turbines that generate electricity. Today, a single 25-megawatt generating plant is providing a significant proportion of the electricity consumed on the Big Island, Hawaii. In the 1980s, The Geysers field in California was producing almost 2000 megawatts, although this figure has now declined by about 40 per cent. Pumping water into the ground in regions of hot dry rock to generate steam artificially is a technique that may prove to be a valuable energy source in the future.

Tourism

Volcanoes have always attracted attention. Eruptions, geysers and hot springs are spectacular sights, but even the esthetically pleasing conical shape of a dormant or extinct volcano can draw visitors to marvel at the beauty of nature. In Japan, Mount Fuji is an object of veneration in the Shinto religion whose followers worship nature in all its forms. The

Geothermal energy is a byproduct of volcanic activity and it can be harnessed to
provide power and hot water. This has been done extensively in Iceland where the capital,
Reykjavik, is heated by natural hot water. A large open-air swimming pool, naturally heated, has
been created in the blue lagoon adjacent to the geothermal power plant.

Romans knew Vulcano, the Italian island from which our word 'volcano' is derived, as the forge of Vulcan, their god of weapons. Even in Antarctica, tourists are still thrilled by the sight of Mount Erebus that so excited James Clark Ross 160 years ago. In the South Shetland Islands, off the northwest coast of the Antarctic Peninsula, parties regularly climb to the summit of Penguin Island to walk around the perfect crater and see the small parasitic cone in its center. A short distance away, inside the caldera of Deception Island, they can join the Antarctic Swimming Club in Pendulum Cove where submarine springs just offshore keep the water at a pleasant temperature. Compared with other parts of the world, the British Isles enjoy relative freedom from the natural hazards of earthquakes and volcanoes, but this has not always been so. They existed so long ago that they are no longer recognizable by their shape, only by the rocks themselves. The most spectacular evidence of former volcanoes can still be seen in the fantastic columnar basalt lavas of the Giant's Causeway in County Antrim in Northern Ireland, a popular tourist attraction. These hexagonal columns were formed as the cooling lava contracted.

A geyser in the volcanic area of Rotorua, New Zealand.

In the United States, the Old Faithful geyser has been a popular tourist venue ever since the Yellowstone area was established as the first of America's national parks in 1872. There is no doubt that visitors to volcanic areas will continue to underwrite the tourist industry for generations to come.

The Giant's Causeway, an ancient lava flow with spectacular hexagonal columns.

Predicting Eruptions

Thermal Activity

Perhaps the most obvious indicator of a forthcoming eruption is the increase of thermal activity. This is something that can usually be easily observed without the use of sophisticated instrumentation. When the temperature of the underlying magma chamber increases there may be a change in fumarolic activity or in the temperature of hot springs. Geyser eruptions may become more frequent and more vigorous. There may be an increase in the amount of steam issuing from an existing crater and sometimes, as often happens with Hawaiian volcanoes, a lava lake will start to develop in the crater. All these features are indications that changes are taking place beneath the volcano and they may presage an eruption. If the volcano has a well-documented history of recent eruptions it is likely that a pattern of activity will have emerged so that volcanologists can begin to estimate the likelihood of an eruption and possibly its magnitude. However, it is still very difficult to forecast just when the eruption will occur. Volcanoes can be fickle and will not always follow the predicted pattern.

The eruption of Mount St Helens in the Cascade Range of the Rocky Mountains in Washington State was one of the most closely monitored and well-documented eruptions of all time. Activity was first noticed on 20 March 1980 but the cataclysmic eruption did not happen until 18 May 1980 and it did so with no immediate warning. Although the increasing activity had been watched carefully, there was no indication how far the activity would continue to increase before it could no longer be contained. It is interesting to note that geologists who had been studying the previous eruption cycles of the volcano suggested in 1978 that the former 1000-year periodicity of major eruptions was unlikely to run its full term this time. They predicted the next major eruption would occur within the next 100 years or possibly before the end of the twentieth century. Little did they realize the eruption was just two years away.

A close view of lava fountains on the Big Island of Hawaii.

Seismic Activity

The first stages in the development of an eruption involve the movement of magma in the chamber below the volcano. The magma becomes hotter and tries to expand, gases move through the magma trying to escape from the chamber, and magma from deeper in the crust or in the mantle is trying to move upward; all these place increasing pressure on the structure of the volcano and the structure will adjust to compensate for these pressure changes. Solid rock is often brittle so that unless it is totally confined, it tends to break, rather than bend, and when it breaks, the shock wave creates a seismic disturbance. At first these disturbances are likely to be small and detectable only by sensitive seismometers, but as the pressure from beneath increases the disturbances will grow in strength and become more frequent. Geophysicists can monitor the growing strength of the seismic activity and predict that an eruption is due but they cannot tell when it will happen, only that it almost certainly *will* happen.

China has a long history of earthquakes and, as early as AD 132, the Chinese philosopher Zhang Heng designed a primitive but effective and remarkably sensitive seismometer, or earthquake detector. It comprised a heavy pendulum suspended inside a large bronze container. The pendulum was connected by simple levers to the movable jaws of eight dragons on the outside. In each mouth there was a small ball and when the pendulum was moved, the jaws of one of the dragons would open and release the ball which fell into the open mouth of a bronze toad. The direction of the earthquake could be determined by which dragon had released its ball. A modern seismometer is a miniaturized sophisticated electronic instrument that is so sensitive that it must be placed on a very solid foundation, well away from local disturbances such as roads and railways, so that it can distinguish between true seismic disturbances and the movement of local traffic.

Physical Deformity

The volcanoes on the Big Island of Hawaii are in almost continuous activity so are closely monitored in order to predict when a major eruption may occur. One type of instrument that is used to give advance warning is a tiltmeter. In essence, this is a very

The basalt lavas of Hawaiian volcanoes are particularly hot and fluid. This allows them to flow very fast for considerable distances, sometimes several miles, so that some flows reach the sea and are still red-hot when they do so. The sea may actually boil where the lava enters the water and this creates a steamy inferno. Conversely, beneath the water, the lava is being rapidly chilled and separates into 'blobs' up to 3 ft (90 cm) across. These roll down the slope and eventually accumulate into heaps of 'pillows'. Despite being chilled they are not solid but can still change shape; each pillow usually develops a keel where the overlying pillow spreads downward into the gap between the pillows beneath it. Pillow structure is readily recognizable and indicates that a lava flow cooled underwater. This is a particularly valuable feature for a geologist who is trying to determine the environment of an ancient eruption.

sensitive spirit level that is positioned on the flank of the volcano. In practice, several tiltmeters are positioned in strategic locations. As the pressure of magma grows inside the volcano the whole mountain will begin to swell very slightly to accommodate this. The tiltmeters are sufficiently sensitive to record very small changes that can indicate to geologists that an eruption is approaching. They will not be able to tell just when the eruption will happen but the tiltmeters may give a good indication of where the volcano is most likely to rupture and which way the lava is most likely to flow. Warnings can then be issued and suitable precautions taken to minimize the potential loss of life and damage to property.

Despite all the sophisticated technology that scientists can use to monitor and record volcanic activity, and despite all the knowledge of previous activity that geologists can interpret from studying volcanic rocks, it is still not possible to predict accurately when a volcano will erupt. The best forecast they are able to give from the available evidence is that a volcano will erupt, that it will most likely erupt in a certain place and in a particular direction, and they can estimate the likely size of the eruption. Even so, they cannot always be right in these predictions and are often taken by surprise. The civil authorities with the responsibility for the safety of the local population also have a dilemma. They must consider the advice of the scientists and make a decision that will avoid evacuating an area too soon or unnecessarily, but that will also ensure that the affected area has been evacuated when the eruption occurs. They have to act in the knowledge that there is a better than even chance that their decision will be wrong.

Folklore

Many people believe that some animals possess a 'sixth sense' that can warn them of impending disasters. While it is undoubtedly true that animals are much more closely in tune with nature than civilized mankind, there is no scientific evidence that they can predict volcanic eruptions. If it is true, then it is possible that mankind could also have done so in the past. However, man has now certainly lost that ability as he has become increasingly 'civilized' and more reliant on technology than instinct.

A marine iguana, apparently oblivious to the steam from a lava flow entering the sea at Cape Hammond in the Galapagos Islands.

Legend:
- ● featured volcanoes
- plate boundary and ocean ridge
- plate boundary and subduction zone
- plate boundary and collision zone
- plate boundary uncertain
- ➤ movement of plates

Beerenberg

Eldfjell
Grimsvötn
Mt Hekla
Laki
Surtsey

NORTH AMERICAN PLATE

EURASIAN PLATE

Mid Atlantic Ridge

Vesuvius

Stromboli

Vulcano

Mt Etna

Santorini

ARABIAN PLATE

CARIBBEAN PLATE

COCOS PLATE

Mt Pelée

AFRICAN PLATE

SOMALI PLATE

Carlsberg Ridge

Cotopaxi

Kimanura

Longonot

NAZCA PLATE

East Pacific Ridge

SOUTH AMERICAN PLATE

Mid Atlantic Ridge

Central Indian Ridge

Tristan da Cunha

Southwest Indian Ridge

ANTARCTIC PLATE

Katmai
Mt Megeil

Novarupta
Shishaldin

Karymsky

Kliuchevskoi

JUAN DE
FUCA
PLATE

Mt St Helens

NORTH
AMERICAN
PLATE

Mt Fuji

Mt Pinatubo

PHILIPPINE
PLATE

Mauna Loa
Kilauea

PACIFIC
PLATE

Paricutin

Pacaya

COCOS
PLATE

Krakatoa
nak Krakatoa

Mt Bromo
Semeru

INDO-AUSTRALIAN
PLATE

NAZCA
PLATE

Southeast Indian Ridge

Mt Ruapehu

Mt Erebus
approx
1000 miles
(1700 km)
this way

ANTARCTIC   PLATE

Famous Volcanic Eruptions

Mount St Helens

The Cascade Range in the western states of Washington and Oregon in the U.S.A. includes several active volcanoes. They form part of the Pacific 'Ring of Fire' and are fueled by the subduction of the Juan de Fuca plate beneath the western seaboard of the United States. Mount St Helens was known from isolated accounts by explorers to have erupted in the period 1831-57 but it had been peaceful since then, so nobody anticipated an imminent eruption. The first indication of any activity came on 20 March 1980 with several minor earthquakes at shallow depths beneath the northern flank of the mountain. Two days later there were small explosions of steam from a new crater about 230 ft (70 m) across on the snow-capped summit. The crater continued to grow, forming a hole some 1640 ft by 985 ft (500 by 300 m) across and 650 ft (200 m) deep beneath a column of gas and ash that rose 2 miles (3 km) into the atmosphere. The shape of the mountain was also distorting and by 12 April the bulge of the north side had moved outwards about 328 ft (100 m) and covered an area 1¼ miles (2 km) in diameter. Study of a series of photographs showed that the bulge was growing at about 5 ft (1.5 m) per day, directly above the earthquake zone. All this information indicated that an eruption was nigh but it was impossible to estimate when it would occur

Cataclysmic eruption of Mount St Helens.

Mount St Helens and Spirit Lake, Washington State, showing forests devastated by the 1980 eruption.

or how violent it might be. At 8.32 AM on 18 May 1980 the climax occurred.

An earthquake of magnitude 5 released the pressure on the shallow magma chamber allowing dissolved gases to escape. This triggered two major landslides on the north side of the mountain, allowing heated groundwater to flash into steam and the magma to erupt explosively. These combined forces shot a mixture of steam and debris at temperatures up to 572°F (300°C) in a lateral blast to the north at speeds of up to 621 mph (1000 kmph). Total destruction occurred for 20 miles (30 km) from the mountain over an area of 230 sq miles (600 sq km). Trees up to 6 ft 6 in (2 m) in diameter were uprooted, stripped of their branches and left lying like heaps of toothpicks. A vertical eruption followed forcing a debris cloud 16 miles (26 km) into the atmosphere. The worst was over in five minutes but nearly 20 years on, a new lava dome is growing in the new crater.

Santorini

The island of Thera or Santorini lies in the eastern Mediterranean north of Crete. Today it is a holiday destination, where an attractive Greek town perches precariously on an oddly shaped island. To one side the bathymetry of the nautical charts shows a broadly circular structure, 30 sq miles (80 sq km) in area, in the contours of the sea floor. The clue to its origin lies in the continuing volcanic activity; the last eruption in 1950 formed a lava dome and thick lava flows on some of the nearby islands. The circular structure is an ancient caldera that formed about 3500 years ago. The eruption that caused this caldera must have been similar to the eruption of Krakatoa. The extent of the ash fall, estimated from sediment cores taken from the sea floor in the surrounding region, covered an elliptical area about 215 miles (350 km) wide from about 90 miles (150 km) northwest of the island to about 435 miles (700 km) to the southeast.

In many ways the eruption of Santorini was just another major eruption in history and of geological interest only. However, many people believe that it may have been the source of the legendary lost continent of Atlantis. The cataclysmic eruption destroyed the Minoan civilization of the eastern Mediterranean that was centered on Crete in the Late Bronze Age. In about 590 BC a Greek named Solon traveled to Egypt where he learned from local

Part of the rim of the ancient volcano of Santorini in the eastern Mediterranean Sea. The eruption of the volcano about 3500 years ago resulted in the collapse of the central part into the underlying magma chamber, so that only parts of the original crater rim remain, as a circle of islands.

historians that a disaster had struck the people of Keftiu in ancient times. This was a place far to the west that has been tentatively identified as Minoan Crete. In about 380 BC, the Greek philosopher Plato developed Solon's story into what has become the legend of Atlantis.

Krakatoa

Krakatoa, or Krakatau, was a small uninhabited volcanic island in the Sunda Strait between Java and Sumatra. Volcanic activity began with small ash explosions on 20 May 1883, the first known activity since 1680. On 27 May scientists who visited found that much of the vegetation had been killed by volcanic ash. There were also some blocks of pumice floating in the sea. The volcano quietened until late June when two columns of steam were observed. The island was visited again on 11 August when three active vents were reported. On 26 August 1883, the activity renewed with dramatic intensity. At 1 PM noises like thunder were heard up to 125 miles (200 km) away and by 2 PM a black cloud had developed over the island to a height of 17 miles (27 km). Darkness descended and at 10 AM the next day there was an enormous explosion followed about half an hour later by tsunamis running ashore around the coasts. At 10.50 AM there was a second big explosion but the explosions diminished during the next few days and the activity finally ceased in October.

The magnitude of the eruption becomes apparent when you start to analyze what actually happened. The main explosion at 10 AM was heard 3000 miles (4800 km) away in Australia like the sound of distant cannons, the loudest noise ever heard by human ears. The tsunamis killed more than 36,000 people. The eruption produced 18 cubic ft of pumice that covered thousands of square miles; where previously the peak of Danan had been 1500 ft (450 m) high there was now ocean 660 ft (200 m) deep; about 4 cubic miles (6 cubic km) of the island had disappeared and the fine ash ejected into the atmosphere was distributed around the globe, causing spectacularly colored sunsets for two or three years. In 1927 a new island Anak Krakatau (son of Krakatoa) appeared and continues to grow. Krakatoa is not yet dead.

An eruption of Anak Krakatoa, a new volcano emerging from the submerged crater of Krakatoa.

Mount Pinatubo

The eruption of Mount Pinatubo on Luzon island in the Philippines in 1991 is a good example of rapid geological research from a position of almost total ignorance, effective educational publicity and cooperative authorities being combined to avert a major human disaster. Before the eruption sequence began hardly anybody realized that Mount Pinatubo was a volcano. There was no local memory of volcanic activity and the mountain, clothed in thick jungle, did not even look like a volcano. In March 1991 a swarm of small earthquakes alerted scientists at the Philippine Volcanic Institute who immediately began to monitor the activity. With colleagues from the U.S. Geological Survey they made a rapid reconnaissance of the region and showed that there had been major explosive eruptions that had produced enormous ashflows and lahars about 5500, 3000 and 500 years ago. The activity progressed quickly and in May the volcano was producing more than 5000 tons of sulfur dioxide gas each day. In early June there were small ash explosions followed by the development of a lava dome that produced a column of steam and ash 4 miles (7 km) high.

Satellite image of Mount Pinatubo in the Philippines.

The potential for a human catastrophe was very high so an educational program was shown widely to advise people of the dangers to come. A film of volcanic eruptions was shown to all sections of the population, particularly to the civil authorities. Its message was well taken. By 14 June some 75,000 people had been evacuated from within a radius of 20 miles (30 km) from the summit. On 15 June colossal explosions produced a cloud of ash about 21 miles (34 km) high and 250 miles (400 km) wide. Unfortunately, direct

The summit crater of Longonot volcano in Kenya.

Summit of dormant Cotopaxi in the Andes of Ecuador.

Mount Bromo in Indonesia, gently simmering.

The caldera of Mauna Loa, Hawaii.

The crater within the summit cone of Mount Megeik, one of several active
volcanoes in the Katmai region of Alaska. The original Valley of Ten Thousand Smokes
is now cold but the volcanic activity of the region continues.

observation of the eruption was largely prevented by the arrival of Typhoon Yunya which added heavy rainfall to the chaos and fueled lahars that swept down the mountain in all directions. The main eruption lasted about three hours and left high-temperature ash deposits up to 650 ft (200 m) thick. The U.S. Clark Air Base was almost completely destroyed but amazingly, thanks to the evacuation organized by cooperative authorities, only 300 people lost their lives. Most of them were killed when roofs collapsed under the weight of wet ash; without the heavy rain the death toll might have been much less.

Parícutin

About 220 miles (350 km) west of Mexico City, farmers in a valley had been intrigued by a small pit that appeared in a field. No matter how often they filled it with earth it would still reappear. On 20 February 1943, soon after 4 PM, a column of gray volcanic ash began to spout from a fissure that had developed across the pit. A day later lava began to erupt from the base of a cone of ash and volcanic debris that was already 165 ft (50 m) high. The new volcano continued to grow rapidly as more lava was produced and piled on top of earlier lava flows. Within a few months the inhabitants of Parícutin village 2 miles (3 km) away were forced to evacuate their homes and by June 1944 the district town of San Juan Parangacutiro had been overrun by lava and destroyed. The volcano continued to grow until by September 1944 it had covered an area of 25 sq miles (9½ sq km).

The activity continued for two years by which time the volcano had reached its maximum height of 1650 ft (500 m). Most of the 1690 cubic yards (1.3 cu km) of volcanic ash and the 910 cubic yards (0.7 cu km) of lava were produced in this time. The activity gradually waned until it ceased abruptly early in 1952. It had been just over nine years from its birth to its death and this was the first time that the complete lifecycle of a volcano had ever been observed scientifically.

Katmai

The northern section of the Pacific 'Ring of Fire' is formed by the volcanoes of the Aleutian Islands and the Alaskan Peninsula where the Pacific plate is being subducted in a north-

northeasterly direction. In 1912, magma began to accumulate beneath Katmai volcano but when the eruption came it was not through the existing crater but through side fissures about 6 miles (10 km) away. There were three huge explosions, heard as far away as 600 miles (950 km), that signalled the main eruption, which lasted about two days and produced a total of 7 cubic miles (30 cu km) of ash. A large part of this emerged as a pyroclastic flow that filled a valley 12½ miles (16 km) long by 2 miles (3 km) wide with up to 650 ft (200 m) of hot ash. The fallout of ash from the eruption cloud covered a much larger area and in the town of Kodiak, 100 miles (160 km) to the south, the darkness created was so intense that people reported being unable to see a lantern held at arm's length. The quantity of fine ash in the air made breathing difficult and potentially harmful. Although the eruption site, called Novarupta, was so far from the center of the volcano, the magma chamber itself was located beneath the summit of Katmai and, once the chamber had been drained, the original crater collapsed into the void and created a caldera 4 miles (6 km) wide and 2600 ft (800 m) deep.

The valley of hot ash retained its heat for many years and percolating groundwater escaped as steam through countless fumaroles; it became known as the Valley of Ten Thousand Smokes. The fumaroles are mostly dead now but a new vent on the west side of Katmai, Mount Trident, has produced several lava flows and last erupted in 1974.

Hawaii

The Hawaiian islands stretch west-northwest across the central Pacific Ocean from the island of Hawaii itself (the Big Island) for some 1250 miles (2000 km) to the island of Kure. They are not formed by volcanism at a mid-ocean ridge; their origin lies in a mantle plume or hot spot whose source is deep in the mantle, possibly as deep as the core–mantle boundary. Hot spots are long-lived stationary features and it is the ocean crust moving over the hot spot that has created the chain of volcanic islands. The lavas on Kure are about 27.7 million years old and most of the lavas on the Big Island are less than 400,000 years old. The current movement of the Pacific plate is calculated at about 3½ in (9 cm) per year and a new submarine feature called Loih has been recorded to the southeast of the Big Island,

The Puu Oo center that lies along the eastern rift zone of Kilauea volcano on the Big Island of Hawaii is one of the principal active vents in recent years. The picture shows the cinder cone built from continual ash eruptions. Many of these ash eruptions formed spectacular lava fountains, some shooting skyward as much as 1300 ft (400 m), creating one of nature's most dramatic firework displays. Lava from the volcano, seen here in the foreground, has flowed some 4½ miles (7 km) to the sea. Successive flows pouring into the sea have extended the coastline into the ocean along a 9 mile (15 km) front, adding more than ¾ mile (2 sq km) of new land to the island. Puu Oo is one of several small volcanoes that have erupted within the main caldera of Kilauea.

The 1973 eruption of Eldfjell on Heimaey in the Vestmann Islands off the south coast of Iceland. Although the town was evacuated and many houses destroyed, the harbor was spared and the islanders were able to return and continue their main occupation of fishing.

indicating that the plate is still moving and that the hot spot is still active.

Mauna Loa and Kilauea are the best known of the five major volcanoes on the Big Island. Kilauea has been in almost continuous eruption since 1983 but perhaps the most spectacular sight is the Halemaumau lava lake in the main caldera. It is about half a mile (1 km) across and frequently produces many lava fountains. The low viscosity of the lava ensures that the eruptions are not explosive on the scale of many other volcanoes so they are much more predictable. The lava is very hot and flows for considerable distances, doing extensive damage but rarely endangering life. Often the surface of a flow will cool sufficiently to form a crust, like the skin on custard, and its undulating surface is known as pahoehoe. Sometimes the surface is wrinkled. Lava surfaces that are more fragmented and broken into blocks are known as aa. The crust on pahoehoe may allow the fluid lava below to drain away as the eruption dies, leaving lava tunnels beneath the surface.

The Big Island volcanoes have been observed by scientists at the Hawaiian Volcano Observatory since 1912, making them the most closely studied volcanoes in the world.

Iceland

Iceland is a totally volcanic island that sits astride the Mid-Atlantic Ridge. There are many volcanic islands along and close to the ridge, from Beerenberg on Jan Mayen, the northernmost active volcano in the world, to Tristan da Cunha in the South Atlantic, but Iceland is by far the largest. The reason for this is that Iceland also lies over a hot spot, but because the hot spot is stationary beneath the spreading center, Iceland continues to grow as its two sides move apart on the spreading ridge and new magma rises to fill the gap. Geologists use chemical analysis to distinguish between the lavas originating in the upper mantle from sea-floor spreading and those from the lower mantle hot spot source. Remnants of the original Icelandic volcanic province can be seen today on the opposing shores of southeast Greenland and northwest Scotland and some geologists believe that hot-spot activity and mantle plumes may initiate continental break-up and sea-floor spreading.

Many different volcanic features can be seen in Iceland, which is not surprising for an island that has few other rocks. The most impressive eruptions have been from fissures that trend roughly southwest–northeast across the island, reflecting the activity of the underlying ridge. In fact Iceland is slowly and continuously splitting apart as new lava is injected into the crust from below. The eruption from the Laki fissure in 1783 produced a lava flow 40-43 miles (65-70 km) long, the longest in historic times, although longer flows are known from the geological record, such as the Pomona flow in Washington State, U.S.A., some 15 million years ago, that was about 310 miles (500 km) long. Perhaps the most exciting event in recent years was when the crew of a fishing boat near the Vestmann Islands observed a column of ash rising about 200 ft (60 m) from the surface of the sea about a mile (1.5 km) away. It was 7.30 AM on 14 November 1963 and they were seeing the very start of the eruption that was eventually to become the island of Surtsey. In 1973, an eruption of the nearby island of Heimaey forced the 5000 inhabitants to evacuate the town as more than 200 houses were buried in ash. The lava stopped just before closing the harbor entrance.

Mont Pelée

The island of Martinique in the West Indies is part of the volcanic island arc formed by subduction of the Atlantic sea floor as it sinks westward beneath the islands. Its volcanic character is therefore similar to that of many of the volcanoes that constitute the Pacific 'Ring of Fire' because it has a similar geological setting. On 23 April 1902 the volcano of Mont Pelée at the northern end of the island began emitting gas and ash to such an extent that in the streets of St Pierre, 6 miles (10 km) to the south, animals were dying of suffocation by the poisonous fumes. In the face of this activity it would have been prudent to evacuate the town but an important election was due and voters could only cast their votes in their home towns, so few people moved. The explosions continued and mudflows poured from the crater from 5 to 7 May, killing a number of people, but still no-one moved. At 7.50 AM on 8 May the main eruption occurred and a *nuée ardente* overflowed from the crater down the valley of the Rivière Blanche. It turned away from the town towards the sea and filled the valley with thick deposits of ignimbrite. However, ahead of the ash cloud was a fast-moving surge of gas and suspended ash and this was not deflected; it enveloped St Pierre, killing all but two or three of the town's 30,000 inhabitants in a matter of seconds.

*A lake formed within the crater of an inactive volcano in Iceland has become
a natural swimming pool. Most such lakes in Iceland are quite safe and may even contain
warm water, heated by the residual activity of the volcano. However, in some other parts of
the world, crater lakes may contain a rich cocktail of dissolved volcanic gases, making
the lake, in effect, a pool of sulfuric and other acids.*

A satellite image of part of the Kamchatka Peninsula in easternmost Russia showing clearly the conical shape of the snow-covered Kliuchevskoi volcano. Satellite images have proved invaluable to geologists because they allow major geological structures to be shown in a single picture.

One of the survivors was a convict in the jail where he was moderately well-protected.

The temperature of the gas was sufficient to melt metal and glass and led the geologist, Alfred Lacroix, to introduce the term *nuée ardente* (glowing cloud) for this type of cloud eruption. Similar eruptions continued in the following months, mostly less destructive than the original blast, and the final event was the growth of a lava dome and spine. Gradually the spine crumbled away and the volcano grew quiet as it gathered strength for the next eruption. Three further explosive eruptions have been recorded, the last in 1932.

Vesuvius

In AD 63 a violent earthquake shook the area around Vesuvius, damaging the surrounding towns. Smaller earthquakes continued for several years but nobody paid much attention and certainly did not connect the activity with Vesuvius. The Romans knew that Vesuvius was a volcano but there was no record of any eruptions and they were sure that it was extinct; today such activity would be regarded as

The summit crater of Mount Vesuvius, seen from an aeroplane.

warning of an impending eruption. Sixteen years later, on 24 August 79, the volcano finally exploded and the column of ash was carried by the wind for 60 miles (100 km) to the south, overwhelming the town of Pompeii and its inhabitants. Herculaneum was also destroyed but recent research has suggested that it was not by mudflows, as had previously been thought, but by a flow of incandescent ash such as a *nuée ardente*. The eruption was described in graphic detail by the Roman historian Pliny the Younger in a letter to Tacitus and as such is probably the first written account of a volcanic eruption. He likened the ash cloud to an Italian pine tree, the oval flattened crowns of such trees being of a very similar shape to the ash cloud.

Eruptions of Vesuvius have continued intermittently ever since and there have been more than 50 during the following 1920 years. Most of these eruptions begin with an explosive ash cloud followed by lava flows. The last eruption was in 1944.

Italians have had to learn to live with volcanoes. Stromboli, off the southwest coast, has been in almost continuous eruption for more than 2000 years; regular explosions of incandescent lava from the summit crater have earned it the name of 'Lighthouse of the Mediterranean'. Vulcano is less active but has erupted about ten times in the past 2200 years. Mount Etna, on the island of Sicily, tends to have rather more violent eruptions from its summit crater. The first recorded activity was as long ago as 1500 BC, since when it has produced lava flows on more than 150 occasions, the last being in 1996. These eruptions can be particularly devastating for farmers who grow vines on the rich volcanic soils. The benefit of the fertile soil has always to be weighed against the risk of destruction by lava.

Conclusions

Volcanoes are a constant reminder that we live on an active planet. They invoke emotions from veneration to sheer horror. Whatever our emotions, volcanoes never fail to impress with their awesome power, putting man's technological achievements into perspective in relation to nature. We cannot reliably predict eruptions nor can we control them; we can only watch in amazement as they pursue their courses.

To the geologist, volcanoes provide a window into the deeper levels of the Earth's crust and into the mantle itself. Biologists marvel at the speed of recolonization by plants and animals of land that has been totally devastated. And for the rest of us, it is easy to forget that so many of the materials that we take for granted originated deep within the Earth and have been brought within our reach by volcanoes. Whatever our views and emotions, the Earth would be a much less fascinating place without them.

Moonrise at sunset over Mount St Helens, now peace has returned to the region after the eruption.

The islands of Indonesia form part of the western arm of the Pacific 'Ring of Fire' and many of them contain active volcanoes. Subduction of Pacific Ocean crust westward beneath the islands gives rise to these volcanoes. The summit ash cone of Semeru, towards the eastern end of Java, shows deep gullies eroded by torrential rain during the 1992 eruption.

Glossary

Aa	a lava flow with a 'blocky' surface.
Andesite	a viscous lava erupted from volcanoes above subduction zones.
Basalt	a very fluid, hot and dense lava, the common lava produced at mid-ocean ridges.
Bomb	a fragment of molten lava ejected from the volcano.
Caldera	a large volcanic crater that may be created by explosive ejection of the center of the volcano, or caused by the collapse of the volcano into the underlying magma chamber at the end of the eruption.
Fumarole	a vent that allows volcanic gases to escape from the Earth.
Geothermal	heat from the Earth.
Geyser	a natural fountain of hot water that spouts intermittently.
Hot spot	a deep-seated and stationary source of volcanism, probably at or close to the core–mantle boundary.
Igneous rock	rock that has crystallized from a molten state.
Ignimbrite	the rock formed from a *nuée ardente*.
Jökulhlaup	a flash flood caused by an eruption beneath an ice cap.
Lahar	a river of mud, ash and water released by an eruption.
Lava lake	a 'lake' of molten rock.
Lava	molten or semi-molten rock issuing from a volcano.
Magma	molten rock.
Mantle	the hot, semi-molten layer of the Earth between the crust and the core.
Nuée ardente	a fast-moving suspension of incandescent ash.
Pahoehoe	a lava flow with an undulating surface that may have a ropy appearance.
Pillow lava	a flattened ball of lava erupted into water.
Pumice	a very 'frothy' lava that floats on water.
Plate tectonics	theory that the Earth's crust forms a series of 'plates' that move across the Earth's surface.
Pyroclastic flow	a major flow of volcanic ash down the side of a volcano but less devastating than a *nuée ardente*.
Rift valley	a major break in the continental crust marked by volcanism; a rift valley may eventually develop into a new ocean.
Seismometer	a sensitive instrument for measuring earth tremors and earthquakes.
Subduction zone	the zone where two plates converge and one sinks beneath the other.
Tsunami	a seismic sea wave.
Trench	a deep depression in the ocean floor at the entry to the subduction zone.
Tufa	a rock formed by precipitation of mineral salts from water.
Volcanic ash	small to minute fragments of volcanic rock deposited from an eruption cloud.

Index

Entries in **bold** *indicate pictures*

Recommended Reading and Biographical Note

There are many excellent books on volcanoes that range from specialist academic texts through 'coffee table' volumes of spectacular photographs and books dealing with specific volcanic regions, to introductory texts for the general reader published by geological museums and institutes. Some representative titles are given below. Cattermole, P., *Building planet Earth; five billion years of Earth history.* Cambridge, Cambridge University Press, 2000. Decker, R and Decker, B. *Volcanoes.* (3rd edition.) New York, W H Freeman and Company, 1997. Francis, P., *Volcanoes: a planetary perspective.* Oxford, Oxford University Press, 1993. Krafft, M., *Volcanoes: Fire from the Earth.* London, Thames and Hudson, 1993.

There are also some informative and colorful websites:

World volcanoes

Smithsonian Global Volcanism Program
http://www.volcano.si.edu/gvp/
Volcano World (University of North Dakota)
http://volcano.und.nodak.edu/

Icelandic volcanoes

Nordic Volcanological Institute
http://www.norvol.hi.is/

Italian volcanoes

Instituto Internazionale di Vulcanologia Catania
http://www.iiv.ct.cnr.it/

Japanese volcanoes

Hakone Volcano Research Center
http://hakone.eri.u-tokyo.ac.jp/index.html

Volcanoes in the United States

United States Geological Survey
http://volcanoes.usgs.gov/
Yellowstone National Park
http://www.wku.edu/www/geoweb/geyser.htm

Peter Clarkson is presently the Executive Secretary of the Scientific Commission on Antarctic Research based at the Scott Polar Research Institute in Cambridge. Before that he worked for 22 years as a geologist for the British Antarctic Survey. He has published many popular accounts on volcanoes, most recently for Reader's Digest.